The Complete Air Fryer Cookbook for Family and Friends

Quick and Delicious Recipes for Every Day

Nora T. Coleman

Copyright 2018 by Anthony N. Lowe
All rights reserved. All rights Reserved. No part of this publication or the information in it may be quoted from or reproduced in any form by means such as printing, scanning, photocopying or otherwise without prior written permission of the copyright holder. Disclaimer and Terms of Use: Effort has been made to ensure that the information in this book is accurate and complete, however, the author and the publisherdo not warrant the accuracy of the information, text and graphics contained within the book due to the rapidly changing nature of science, research, known and unknown facts and internet. The Author and the publisher do not hold any responsibility for errors, omissions or contrary interpretation of the subject matter herein. This book is presented solely for motivational and informational purposesonly

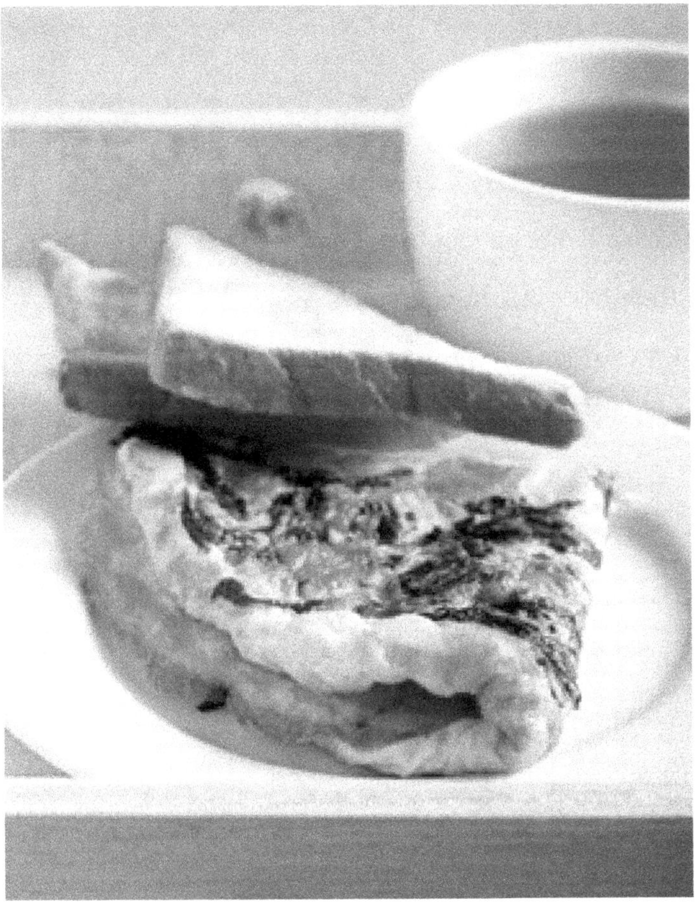

BREAKFAST 8

Mixed Berry Crumble 9

Blackberry and Peach with Vanilla 11 Breaded

Bananas with Chocolate Sauce 13Chocolate

Cinnamon S'mores 15

Simple Coconut Mixed Berry Crisp 16

Chocolate and Blueberry Cupcakes 19

Golden Coconut-Pecan Cookies 21

Lemony Raspberry Muffins 23

Swerve and Cardamon Walnuts Tart 25

LUNCH 27

Air-Fried Beef Bratwursts 28

Mexican Chorizo Scotch Eggs 29

Crunchy Rosemary and Orange Chickpeas 31Fast

Pomegranate Avocado Fries 33

Crunchy Okra Slices 35

Simple Buttery Sweet Potatoes 37

Sweet Corn Fritters 38

Easy Bacon and Green Beans 39

Butternut Squash with Chopped Hazelnuts 40Air-

Fried Shishito Peppers 42

SNACKSPanko-Crusted Tilapia Tacos 43

Crispy Cod Tacos with Salsa 46

Korean Beef and Onion Tacos 48

Curry Shrimp and Zucchini Potstickers 50

Crispy Spinach and Ricotta Pockets 52 Easy

Cheesy Bacon and Egg Wraps 54 Cheesy

Chicken Breasts Wraps 55

MEAT 57

Steak with Brussels Sprouts 58

Barbecue Pork Steaks 60

Cheesy Bacon Burst with Spinach 61

Cheesy Beef and Egg Rolls 63 Cheesy

Beef Chuck Burgers 65

Fast Chicken Fried Steak 66

Crispy Pork Chop 69

Casseroles, Frittatas, and Quiches 71

Sweet Peaches with Yogurt and Blueberries 72

Honey Peaches and Apple Crumble 73

Golden Strawberry and Rhubarb Crisp 75 Fast

Pumpkin Pudding with Vanilla Wafers 77Cocoa

Brownies 79

Easy White Chocolate Cookies 81 Honey-

Lemon Mixed Berry Crisp 83 Golden

Savory Blackberry Muffins 85Mixed Berry

Crumble 87

Breaded Bananas with Chocolate S auce 91

Chocolate Cinnamon S'mores 93

Simple Coconut Mixed Berry Crisp 94

Fast Chocolate Peppermint Cheesecake 95

Chocolate and Blueberry Cupcakes 97 VEGGIE

99

Fast Balsamic Brussels Sprouts 100Ritzy

Summer Rolls 101

Balsamic Rice and Eggplant Bowl 103

Veggies Pizza Squares 105

Cajun Sweet Potatoes with Tofu 106

Cheesy Basmati Risotto 108

Classic Mediterranean Baked Eggs with Spinach 110

BREAKFAST

Mixed Berry Crumble

Prep time: 5 minutes | **Cook time**: 35 minutes | **Serves** 6

2 ounces (57 g) unsweetened mixed berries

½ cup granulated Swerve

2 tablespoons golden flaxseed meal1

teaspoon xanthan gum

½ teaspoon ground cinnamon

¼ teaspoon ground star anise

Topping:

½ stick butter, cut into small pieces1

cup powdered Swerve

⅔ cup almond flour

⅓ cup unsweetened coconut, finely shredded

½ teaspoon baking powder

Cooking spray

1. Coat 6 ramekins with cooking spray.

2. In a mixing dish, stir together the mixed berries, cinnamon,

granulated Swerve, xanthan gum, flaxseed meal, star anise. Divide

the berry mixture evenly among the prepared ramekins.

3. Combine the remaining ingredients in a separate mixing dish and

stir well. Scatter the topping over the berry mixture.

4. Working in batches, place the ramekins in the air fryer basket.

Cook at the corresponding preset mode or Air Fry at 330°F (166°C)

for 35 minutes until the topping is golden brown.

5. Serve warm.

Blackberry and Peach with Vanilla

Prep time: 10 minutes | **Cook time**: 20 minutes | **Serves** 4

Filling:

1 (6-ounce / 170-g) package blackberries

1½ cups chopped peaches, cut into ½-inch thick slices

2 teaspoons arrowroot or cornstarch

2 tablespoons coconut sugar

1 teaspoon lemon juice

Topping:

2 tablespoons sunflower oil

1 tablespoon maple syrup

1 teaspoon vanilla

3 tablespoons coconut sugar

½ cup rolled oats

⅓ cup whole-wheat pastry flour

1 teaspoon cinnamon

¼ teaspoon nutmeg

⅛ teaspoon sea salt

Make the Filling:

1. Combine the peaches, blackberries, arrowroot, coconut sugar, and

lemon juice in a baking pan.

2. Using a rubber spatula, stir until well incorporated. Set aside.

Make the Topping:

3. Combine the oil, maple syrup, and vanilla in a mixing bowl and stir
well. Whisk in the remaining ingredients. Spread this mixtureevenly over the filling.

4. Place the pan in the air fryer basket and cook at the correspondingpreset mode or Air Fry at 320°F (160°C) for 20 minutes, or until
the topping is crispy and golden brown. Serve warm

Breaded Bananas with Chocolate Sauce

Prep time: 10 minutes | **Cook time**: 10 minutes | **Serves** 6

¼ cup cornstarch

¼ cup plain bread crumbs

1 large egg, beaten

3 bananas, halved crosswise

Cooking spray

Chocolate sauce, for serving

1. Place the bread crumbs, cornstarch, and egg in three separate
bowls.
2. Roll the bananas in the cornstarch, then in the beaten egg, and
finally in the bread crumbs to coat well.
3. Spritz the air fryer basket with the cooking spray.
4. Arrange the banana halves in the basket and mist them with the
cooking spray. Cook at the corresponding preset mode orAir Fry at
350°F (177°C) for 5 minutes. Flip the bananas and continueto air
fry for another 2 minutes.

5. Remove the bananas from the basket to a serving plate. Serve with

the chocolate sauce drizzled over the top.

Chocolate Cinnamon S'mores

Prep time: 5 minutes | **Cook time**: 10 minutes | Makes 12 s'mores

12 whole cinnamon graham crackers, halved

2 (1.55-ounce / 44-g) chocolate bars, cut into 12 pieces12 marshmallows

1. Working in batches, arrange 6 graham cracker squares in the air
fryer basket in a single layer.

2. Top each square with a piece of chocolate and bake for 2 minutes.

3. Remove the basket and place a marshmallow on each piece of
melted chocolate. Cook at the corresponding preset mode or Air
Fry at 350°F (177°C) for another 1 minute.

4. Remove from the basket to a serving plate. Repeat with the
remaining 6 graham cracker squares, chocolate pieces, and marshmallows.

5. Serve topped with the remaining graham cracker squares

Simple Coconut Mixed Berry Crisp

Prep time: 5 minutes | **Cook time**: 20 minutes | **Serves** 6

1 tablespoon butter, melted

12 ounces (340 g) mixed berries

⅓ cup granulated Swerve

1 teaspoon pure vanilla extract

½ teaspoon ground cinnamon

¼ teaspoon ground cloves

¼ teaspoon grated nutmeg

½ cup coconut chips, for garnish

1. Coat a baking pan with melted butter.

2. Put the remaining ingredients except the coconut chips in the

prepared baking pan.

3. Cook at the corresponding preset mode or Air Fry at 330°F (166°C)

for 20 minutes.

4. Serve garnished with the coconut chips.Fast Chocolate Peppermint Cheesecake

Prep time: 5 minutes | **Cook time**: 18 minutes | **Serves** 6

Crust:

½ cup butter, melted

½ cup coconut flour

2 tablespoons stevia

Cooking spray

Topping:

4 ounces (113 g) unsweetened baker's chocolate 1

cup mascarpone cheese, at room temperature 1

teaspoon vanilla extract

2 drops peppermint extract

1. Lightly coat a baking pan with cooking spray.

2. In a mixing bowl, whisk together the butter, flour, and stevia until

well combined. Transfer the mixture to the prepared bakingpan.

3. Place the baking pan in the air fryer and cook at the corresponding

preset mode or Air Fry at 350°F (177°C) for 18 minutes untila toothpick inserted in the center comes out clean.

4. Remove the crust from the air fryer to a wire rack to cool.

5. Once cooled completely, place it in the freezer for 20 minutes.

6. When ready, combine all the ingredients for the topping ina small

bowl and stir to incorporate.

7. Spread this topping over the crust and let it sit for another 15 minutes in the freezer.

8. Serve chilled.

Chocolate and Blueberry Cupcakes

Prep time: 5 minutes | **Cook time**: 15 minutes | **Serves** 6

¾ cup granulated erythritol

1¼ cups almond flour

1 teaspoon unsweetened baking powder3

teaspoons cocoa powder

½ teaspoon baking soda

½ teaspoon ground cinnamon

¼ teaspoon grated nutmeg

⅛ teaspoon salt

½ cup milk

1 stick butter, at room temperature

3 eggs, whisked

1 teaspoon pure rum extract

½ cup blueberries

Cooking spray

1. Spray a 6-cup muffin tin with cooking spray.

2. In a mixing bowl, combine the erythritol, cinnamon, nutmeg,

almond flour, cocoa powder, baking powder, baking soda, and salt

and stir until well blended.

3. In another mixing bowl, mix together the milk, butter, egg, and rum extract until thoroughly combined. Slowly and carefully pour this mixture into the bowl of dry mixture. Stir in the blueberries.

4. Spoon the batter into the greased muffin cups, filling each about three-quarters full.

5. Cook at the corresponding preset mode or Air Fry at 345°F (174°C) for 15 minutes, or until the center is springy and a toothpick inserted in the middle comes out clean.

6. Remove from the basket and place on a wire rack to cool. Serve immediately.

Golden Coconut-Pecan Cookies

Prep time: 10 minutes | **Cook time**: 25 minutes | **Serves** 10

1½ cups coconut flour

1½ cups extra-fine almond flour

½ teaspoon baking powder

⅓ teaspoon baking soda

3 eggs plus an egg yolk, beaten

¾ cup coconut oil, at room temperature

1 cup unsalted pecan nuts, roughly chopped

¾ cup monk fruit

¼ teaspoon freshly grated nutmeg

⅓ teaspoon ground cloves

½ teaspoon pure vanilla extract

½ teaspoon pure coconut extract

⅛ teaspoon fine sea salt

1. Line the air fryer basket with parchment paper.

2. Mix the coconut flour, almond flour, baking powder, and baking

soda in a large mixing bowl.

3. In another mixing bowl, stir together the eggs and coconut oil. Add

the wet mixture to the dry mixture.

4. Mix in the remaining ingredients and stir until a soft dough forms.

5. Drop about 2 tablespoons of dough on the parchment paper for
each cookie and flatten each biscuit until it's 1 inch thick.

6. Cook at the corresponding preset mode or Air Fry at 370°F (188°C)
for about 25 minutes until the cookies are golden and firm to the
touch.

7. Remove from the basket to a plate. Let the cookies cool to room
temperature and serve.

Lemony Raspberry Muffins

Prep time: 5 minutes | **Cook time**: 15 minutes | **Serves** 6

2 cups almond flour

¾ cup Swerve

1¼ teaspoons baking powder

⅓ teaspoon ground allspice

⅓ teaspoon ground anise star

½ teaspoon grated lemon zest

¼ teaspoon salt

2 eggs

1 cup sour cream

½ cup coconut oil

½ cup raspberries

1. Line a muffin pan with 6 paper liners.

2. In a mixing bowl, mix the almond flour, baking powder, Swerve,

lemon zest, allspice, anise, and salt.

3. In another mixing bowl, beat the sour cream, eggs, and coconut oil

until well mixed. Add the egg mixture to the flour mixtureand stir

to combine. Mix in the raspberries.

4. Scrape the batter into the prepared muffin cups, filling each about
three-quarters full.

5. Cook at the corresponding preset mode or Air Fry at 345°F (174°C)
for 15 minutes, or until the tops are golden and a toothpick inserted
in the middle comes out clean.

6. Allow the muffins to cool for 10 minutes in the muffin pan before
removing and serving.

Swerve and Cardamon Walnuts Tart

Prep time: 5 minutes | **Cook time**: 13 minutes | **Serves** 6

1 cup coconut milk

½ cup walnuts, ground

½ cup Swerve

½ cup almond flour

½ stick butter, at room temperature

2 eggs

1 teaspoon vanilla essence

¼ teaspoon ground cardamom

¼ teaspoon ground cloves

Cooking spray

1. Coat a baking pan with cooking spray.
2. Combine all the ingredients except the oil in a large bowl and stir until well blended. Spoon the batter mixture into the bakingpan.
3. Cook at the corresponding preset mode or Air Fry at 360°F (182°C) for approximately 13 minutes. Check the tart for doneness: If a toothpick inserted into the center of the tart comes out clean, it's

done.

4. Remove from the air fryer and place on a wire rack to cool. Serve immediately.

LUNCH

Air-Fried Beef Bratwursts

Prep time: 5 minutes | **Cook time**: 15 minutes | **Serves** 4

4 (3-ounce / 85-g) beef bratwursts

1. Place the beef bratwursts in the air fryer basket and cook at the corresponding preset mode or Air Fry at 375°F (191°C) for 15 minutes, turning once halfway through.
2. Serve hot.Fast Air-Fried Asparagus

Prep time: 5 minutes | **Cook time**: 6 minutes | **Serves** 4

1 pound (454 g) asparagus, trimmed and halved crosswise 1 teaspoon extra-virgin olive oil

Salt and pepper, to taste

Lemon wedges, for serving

1. Toss the asparagus with the oil, ⅛ teaspoon salt, and ⅛ teaspoon pepper in bowl. Transfer to air fryer basket.
2. Place the basket in air fryer and cook at the corresponding preset mode or Air Fry at 400°F (204°C) for 6 to 8 minutes, or until tender and bright green, tossing halfway through cooking.
3. Season with salt and pepper and serve with lemon wedges.

Mexican Chorizo Scotch Eggs

Prep time: 5 minutes | **Cook time**: 15 to 20 minutes | Makes 4 eggs

1 pound (454 g) Mexican chorizo or other seasoned sausagemeat

4 soft-boiled eggs plus 1 raw egg1

tablespoon water

½ cup all-purpose flour

1 cup panko bread crumbs

Cooking spray

1. Divide the chorizo into 4 equal portions. Flatten each portion into a
disc. Place a soft-boiled egg in the center of each disc. Wrapthe chorizo around the egg, encasing it completely. Place theencased eggs on a plate and chill for at least 30 minutes.

2. Beat the raw egg with 1 tablespoon of water. Place the flour on a
small plate and the panko on a second plate. Working with 1egg at
a time, roll the encased egg in the flour, then dip it in the egg

mixture. Dredge the egg in the panko and place on a plate. Repeat with the remaining eggs.

3. Spray the eggs with oil and place in the air fryer basket. Cook at the corresponding preset mode or Air Fry at 360°F (182°C) for 10 minutes. Turn and cook for an additional 5 to 10 minutes, oruntil browned and crisp on all sides.

4. Serve immediately.

Crunchy Rosemary and Orange Chickpeas

Prep time: 5 minutes | **Cook time**: 10 to 12 minutes | Makes 4 cups

4 cups cooked chickpeas

2 tablespoons vegetable oil

1 teaspoon kosher salt

1 teaspoon cumin

1 teaspoon paprika

Zest of 1 orange

1 tablespoon chopped fresh rosemary

1. Make sure the chickpeas are completely dry prior to roasting. In a medium bowl, toss the chickpeas with oil, salt, cumin, and paprika.

2. Working in batches, spread the chickpeas in a single layer in the air fryer basket. Cook at the corresponding preset mode or AirFry at 400°F (204°C) for 10 to 12 minutes until crisp, shaking once halfway through.

3. Return the warm chickpeas to the bowl and toss with the orange zest and rosemary. Allow to cool completely.

4. Serve.

Fast Pomegranate Avocado Fries

Prep time: 5 minutes | **Cook time**: 7 to 8 minutes | **Serves** 4

1 cup panko bread crumbs

1 teaspoon kosher salt, plus more for sprinkling1 teaspoon garlic powder

½ teaspoon cayenne pepper

2 ripe but firm avocados

1 egg, beaten with 1 tablespoon water

Cooking spray

Pomegranate molasses, for serving

1. Whisk together the panko, salt, and spices on a plate. Cut each

avocado in half and remove the pit. Cut each avocado half into 4

slices and scoop the slices out with a large spoon, taking careto keep the slices intact.

2. Dip each avocado slice in the egg wash and then dredge itin the

panko. Place the breaded avocado slices on a plate.

3. Working in 2 batches, arrange half of the avocado slices ina single

layer in the air fryer basket. Spray lightly with oil. Cook the slices

at the corresponding preset mode or Air Fry at 375°F (191°C) for 7

to 8 minutes, turning once halfway through. Remove the cooked

slices to a platter and repeat with the remaining avocado slices.

4. Sprinkle the warm avocado slices with salt and drizzle with pomegranate molasses. Serve immediately.

Crunchy Okra Slices

Prep time: 5 minutes | **Cook time**: 8 to 10 minutes | **Serves** 4

1 cup self-rising yellow cornmeal 1 teaspoon Italian-style seasoning 1 teaspoon paprika

1 teaspoon salt

½ teaspoon freshly ground black pepper2 large eggs, beaten

2 cups okra slices

Cooking spray

1. Line the air fryer basket with parchment paper.

2. In a shallow bowl, whisk the cornmeal, Italian-style seasoning, paprika, salt, and pepper until blended. Place the beaten eggsin a second shallow bowl.

3. Add the okra to the beaten egg and stir to coat. Add the egg and okra mixture to the cornmeal mixture and stir until coated.

4. Place the okra on the parchment and spritz it with oil.

5. Cook at the corresponding preset mode or Air Fry at 400°F (204°C)

for 4 minutes. Shake the basket, spritz the okra with oil, and air fry

for 4 to 6 minutes more until lightly browned and crispy.

6. Serve immediately.

Simple Buttery Sweet Potatoes

Prep time: 5 minutes | **Cook time**: 10 minutes | **Serves** 4

2 tablespoons butter, melted

1 tablespoon light brown sugar

2 sweet potatoes, peeled and cut into ½-inch cubes

Cooking spray

1. Line the air fryer basket with parchment paper.

2. In a medium bowl, stir together the melted butter and brown sugar
until blended. Toss the sweet potatoes in the butter mixture until
coated.

3. Place the sweet potatoes on the parchment and spritz with oil.

4. Cook at the corresponding preset mode or Air Fry at 400°F (204°C)
for 5 minutes. Shake the basket, spritz the sweet potatoes with oil,
and air fry for 5 minutes more until they're soft enough to cut witha
fork.

5. Serve immediately.

Sweet Corn Fritters

Prep time: 15 minutes | **Cook time**: 8 minutes | **Serves** 6

1 cup self-rising flour

1 tablespoon sugar

1 teaspoon salt

1 large egg, lightly beaten

¼ cup buttermilk

¾ cup corn kernels

¼ cup minced onion

Cooking spray

1. Line the air fryer basket with parchment paper.

2. In a medium bowl, whisk the flour, sugar, and salt until blended.

Stir in the egg and buttermilk. Add the corn and minced onion.

Mix well. Shape the corn fritter batter into 12 balls.

3. Place the fritters on the parchment and spritz with oil. Cook at the

corresponding preset mode or Air Fry at 350°F (177°C) for 4 minutes. Flip the fritters, spritz them with oil, and cook for 4 minutes more until firm and lightly browned.

4. Serve immediately.

Easy Bacon and Green Beans

Prep time: 15 minutes | **Cook time**: 8 to 10 minutes | **Serves** 4

2 (14.5-ounce / 411-g) cans cut green beans, drained4

bacon slices, air-fried and diced

¼ cup minced onion

1 tablespoon distilled white vinegar

1 teaspoon freshly squeezed lemon juice

½ teaspoon salt

½ teaspoon freshly ground black pepper

Cooking spray

1. Spritz a baking pan with oil. In the prepared pan, stir together the
green beans, onion, bacon, lemon juice, vinegar, salt, andpepper until blended.

2. Place the pan on the air fryer basket.

3. Cook at the corresponding preset mode or Air Fry at 370°F (188°C)
for 4 minutes. Stir the green beans and air fry for 4 to 6 minutes
more until soft.

4. Serve immediately.

Butternut Squash with Chopped Hazelnuts

Prep time: 10 minutes | **Cook time**: 20 minutes | Makes 3 cups

2 tablespoons whole hazelnuts

3 cups butternut squash, peeled, deseeded, and cubed

¼ teaspoon kosher salt

¼ teaspoon freshly ground black pepper2 teaspoons olive oil

Cooking spray

1. Spritz the air fryer basket with cooking spray.

2. Arrange the hazelnuts in the air fryer. Cook at the corresponding

preset mode or Air Fry at 300°F (149°C) for 3 minutes or until soft.

3. Chopped the hazelnuts roughly and transfer to a small bowl. Set

aside.

4. Set the air fryer temperature to 360°F (182°C). Spritz with cooking

spray.

5. Put the butternut squash in a large bowl, then sprinkle with salt and

pepper and drizzle with olive oil. Toss to coat well.

6. Transfer the squash in the air fryer. Cook at the corresponding
preset mode or Air Fry at 360°F (182°C) for 20 minutes or until the
squash is soft. Shake the basket halfway through the frying time.
7. When the frying is complete, transfer the squash onto a plate and
sprinkle with chopped hazelnuts before serving.

Air-Fried Shishito Peppers

Prep time: 5 minutes | **Cook time**: 5 minutes | **Serves** 4

½ pound (227 g) shishito peppers (about 24)1 tablespoon olive oil

Coarse sea salt, to taste

Lemon wedges, for serving

Cooking spray

1. Spritz the air fryer basket with cooking spray.
2. Toss the peppers with olive oil in a large bowl to coat well.
3. Arrange the peppers in the air fryer.
4. Cook at the corresponding preset mode or Air Fry at 400°F (204°C) for 5 minutes or until blistered and lightly charred. Shake the basket and sprinkle the peppers with salt halfway through the cooking time.
5. Transfer the peppers onto a plate and squeeze the lemon wedges on top before serving

SNACKS

Panko-Crusted Tilapia Tacos

Prep time: 20 minutes | **Cook time**: 10 minutes | **Serves** 4

2 tablespoons milk

⅓ cup mayonnaise

¼ teaspoon garlic powder

1 teaspoon chili powder

1½ cups panko breadcrumbs

½ teaspoon salt

4 teaspoons canola oil

1 pound (454 g) skinless tilapia fillets, cut into 3-inch-longand 1-inch-wide

strips

4 small flour tortillas

Lemon wedges, for topping

Cooking spray

1. Spritz the air fryer basket with cooking spray.
2. Combine the milk, garlic powder, mayo, and chili powderin a

bowl. Stir to mix well. Combine the panko with salt and canola oil

in a separate bowl. Stir to mix well.

3. Dredge the tilapia strips in the milk mixture first, then dunk the
strips in the panko mixture to coat well. Shake the excess off.

4. Arrange the tilapia strips in the air fryer. Cook at the corresponding
preset mode or Air Fry at 400°F (204°C) for 5 minutes or until
opaque on all sides and the panko is golden brown. Flip the strips
halfway through. You may need to work in batches to avoid overcrowding.

5. Unfold the tortillas on a large plate, then divide the tilapia strips
over the tortillas. Squeeze the lemon wedges on top before serving.

Crispy Cod Tacos with Salsa

Prep time: 5 minutes | **Cook time**: 15 minutes | **Serves** 4

2 eggs

1¼ cups Mexican beer

1½ cups coconut flour

1½ cups almond flour

½ tablespoon chili powder

1 tablespoon cumin

Salt, to taste

1 pound (454 g) cod fillet, slice into large pieces 4 toasted corn tortillas

4 large lettuce leaves, chopped

¼ cup salsa

Cooking spray

1. Spritz the air fryer basket with cooking spray.

2. Break the eggs in a bowl, then pour in the beer. Whisk to combine

well.

3. Combine the coconut flour, almond flour, chili powder, cumin, and

salt in a separate bowl. Stir to mix well.

4. Dunk the cod pieces in the egg mixture, then shake the excess off

and dredge into the flour mixture to coat well.

5. Arrange the cod in the air fryer. Cook at the corresponding preset mode or Air Fry at 375°F (191°C) for 15 minutes or until golden brown. Flip the cod halfway through the cooking time.

6. Unwrap the toasted tortillas on a large plate, then divide the cod and lettuce leaves on top. Baste with salsa and wrap to serve.

Korean Beef and Onion Tacos

Prep time: 1 hour 15 minutes | **Cook time**: 12 minutes | **Serves** 6

2 tablespoons gochujang

1 tablespoon soy sauce

2 tablespoons sesame seeds

2 teaspoons minced fresh ginger

2 cloves garlic, minced

2 tablespoons toasted sesame oil

2 teaspoons sugar

½ teaspoon kosher salt

1½ pounds (680 g) thinly sliced beef chuck1 medium red onion, sliced

6 corn tortillas, warmed

¼ cup chopped fresh cilantro

½ cup kimchi

½ cup chopped green onions

1. Combine the gochujang, garlic, ginger, sesame seeds, soy sauce,

sesame oil, sugar, and salt in a large bowl. Stir to mix well.

2. Dunk the beef chunk in the large bowl. Press to submerge, then

wrap the bowl in plastic and refrigerate to marinate for at least 1 hour.

3. Remove the beef chunk from the marinade and transfer to the air fryer basket. Add the onion and cook at the corresponding preset mode or Air Fry at 400°F (204°C) for 12 minutes or until well browned. Shake the basket halfway through.

4. Unfold the tortillas on a clean work surface, then divide the fried beef and onion on the tortillas. Spread the kimchi, cilantro, and green onions on top.

5. Serve immediately.

Curry Shrimp and Zucchini Potstickers

Prep time: 35 minutes | **Cook time**: 15 minutes | **Serves** 10

½ pound (227 g) peeled and deveined shrimp, finely chopped

1 medium zucchini, coarsely grated

1 tablespoon fish sauce

1 tablespoon green curry paste

2 scallions, thinly sliced

¼ cup basil, chopped

30 round dumpling wrappers

Cooking spray

1. Combine the chopped shrimp, zucchini, curry paste, scallions, fish sauce, and basil in a large bowl. Stir to mix well.

2. Unfold the dumpling wrappers on a clean work surface, dab a little water around the edges of each wrapper, then scoop up 1 teaspoon of filling in the middle of each wrapper.

3. Make the potstickers: Fold the wrappers in half and press the edges to seal. Spritz the air fryer basket with cooking spray.

4. Transfer 10 potstickers in the basket each time and spritz with

cooking spray.

5. Cook at the corresponding preset mode or Air Fry at 350°F (177°C)

for 5 minutes or until the potstickers are crunchy and lightly browned. Flip the potstickers halfway through. Repeat with remaining potstickers.

6. Serve immediately.

Crispy Spinach and Ricotta Pockets

Prep time: 20 minutes | **Cook time**: 10 minutes per batch | Makes 8 pockets

2 large eggs, divided

1 tablespoon water

1 cup baby spinach, roughly chopped

¼ cup sun-dried tomatoes, finely chopped

1 cup ricotta cheese

1 cup basil, chopped

¼ teaspoon red pepper flakes

¼ teaspoon kosher salt

2 refrigerated rolled pie crusts

2 tablespoons sesame seeds

1. Spritz the air fryer basket with cooking spray.
2. Whisk an egg with water in a small bowl.
3. Combine the spinach, tomatoes, the other egg, basil, ricotta cheese, red pepper flakes, and salt in a large bowl. Whisk to mix well.
4. Unfold the pie crusts on a clean work surface and slice each crust into 4 wedges. Scoop up 3 tablespoons of the spinach mixture on

each crust and leave ½ inch space from edges.

5. Fold the crust wedges in half to wrap the filling and press the edges

with a fork to seal.

6. Arrange the wraps in the air fryer and spritz with cooking spray.

Sprinkle with sesame seeds. Work in 4 batches to avoid overcrowding.

7. Cook at the corresponding preset mode or Air Fry at 380°F (193°C)

for 10 minutes or until crispy and golden. Flip them halfway through.

8. Serve immediately.

Easy Cheesy Bacon and Egg Wraps

Prep time: 15 minutes | **Cook time**: 20 minutes | **Serves** 3

3 corn tortillas

3 slices bacon, cut into strips

2 scrambled eggs

3 tablespoons salsa

1 cup grated Pepper Jack cheese

3 tablespoons cream cheese, divided

Cooking spray

1. Spritz the air fryer basket with cooking spray.

2. Unfold the tortillas on a clean work surface, divide the bacon and eggs in the middle of the tortillas, then spread with salsa andscatter with cheeses. Fold the tortillas over.

3. Work in batches, arrange the tortillas in the air fryer and cook at the corresponding preset mode or Air Fry at 390°F (199°C) for 10 minutes or until the cheeses melt and the tortillas are lightly browned. Flip the tortillas halfway through. Repeat with remaining tortillas.

4. Serve immediately.

Cheesy Chicken Breasts Wraps

Prep time: 30 minutes | **Cook time**: 5 minutes per batch | **Serves** 12

2 large-sized chicken breasts, cooked and shredded

2 spring onions, chopped

10 ounces (284 g) Ricotta cheese

1 tablespoon rice vinegar

1 tablespoon molasses

1 teaspoon grated fresh ginger

¼ cup soy sauce

⅓ teaspoon sea salt

¼ teaspoon ground black pepper, or more to taste

48 wonton wrappers

Cooking spray

1. Combine all the ingredients, except for the wrappers in a large bowl. Toss to mix well.

2. Unfold the wrappers on a clean work surface, then divide and spoon the mixture in the middle of the wrappers.

3. Dab a little water on the edges of the wrappers, then fold the edge

close to you over the filling. Tuck the edge under the filling and

roll up to seal.

4. Arrange the wrapper in the air fryer and spritz with cooking spray.

Cook at the corresponding preset mode or Air Fry at 375°F (191°C)

for in batches for 5 minutes or until lightly browned. Flip the wraps

halfway through.

5. Serve immediately.

MEAT

Steak with Brussels Sprouts

Prep time: 20 minutes | **Cook time**: 15 minutes | **Serves** 4

1 pound (454 g) beef chuck shoulder steak

2 tablespoons vegetable oil

1 tablespoon red wine vinegar1

teaspoon fine sea salt

½ teaspoon ground black pepper

1 teaspoon smoked paprika

1 teaspoon onion powder

½ teaspoon garlic powder

½ pound (227 g) Brussels sprouts, cleaned and halved

½ teaspoon fennel seeds

1 teaspoon dried basil

1 teaspoon dried sage

1. Massage the beef with the vegetable oil, wine vinegar, salt, black
pepper, paprika, onion powder, and garlic powder, coating itwell.
2. Allow to marinate for a minimum of 3 hours.
3. Remove the beef from the marinade and put in the air fryer. Cook
at the corresponding preset mode or Air Fry at 390°F (199°C) for

10 minutes. Flip the beef halfway through.

4. Put the prepared Brussels sprouts in the air fryer along with the
fennel seeds, basil, and sage.

5. Cook everything at the corresponding preset mode or Air Fry at
380°F (193°C) for another 5 minutes.

6. Give them a good stir. Air fry for an additional 10 minutes.

7. Serve immediately.

Barbecue Pork Steaks

Prep time: 5 minutes | **Cook time**: 15 minutes | **Serves** 4

4 pork steaks

1 tablespoon Cajun seasoning

2 tablespoons BBQ sauce

1 tablespoon vinegar1

teaspoon soy sauce

½ cup brown sugar

½ cup ketchup

1. Sprinkle pork steaks with Cajun seasoning.

2. Combine remaining ingredients and brush onto steaks.

3. Add coated steaks to air fryer. Cook at the corresponding preset
mode or Air Fry at 290°F (143°C) for 15 minutes until just browned.

4. Serve immediately.

Cheesy Bacon Burst with Spinach

Prep time: 5 minutes | **Cook time**: 60 minutes | **Serves** 8

30 slices bacon

1 tablespoon Chipotle seasoning

2 teaspoons Italian seasoning

2½ cups Cheddar cheese

4 cups raw spinach

1. Weave the bacon into 15 vertical pieces and 12 horizontal pieces.
Cut the extra 3 in half to fill in the rest, horizontally.
2. Season the bacon with Italian seasoning and Chipotle seasoning.
3. Add the cheese to the bacon.
4. Add the spinach and press down to compress.
5. Tightly roll up the woven bacon.
6. Line a baking sheet with kitchen foil and add plenty of saltto it.
7. Put the bacon on top of a cooling rack and put that on top of the
baking sheet.
8. Cook at the corresponding preset mode or Air Fry at 375°F (191°C)
for 60 minutes.

9. Let cool for 15 minutes before slicing and serving.

Cheesy Beef and Egg Rolls

Prep time: 15 minutes | **Cook time**: 8 minutes | Makes 6 egg rolls

8 ounces (227 g) raw lean ground beef

½ cup chopped onion

½ cup chopped bell pepper

¼ teaspoon onion powder

¼ teaspoon garlic powder

3 tablespoons cream cheese

1 tablespoon yellow mustard

3 tablespoons shredded Cheddar cheese6 chopped dill pickle chips

6 egg roll wrappers

1. In a skillet, add the beef, bell pepper, onion, onion powder, and

garlic powder. Stir and crumble beef until fully cooked, and vegetables are soft.

2. Take skillet off the heat and add mustard, cream cheese, and

Cheddar cheese, stirring until melted.

3. Pour beef mixture into a bowl and fold in pickles.

4. Lay out egg wrappers and divide the beef mixture into each one.

Moisten egg roll wrapper edges with water. Fold sides to the middle and seal with water.

5. Repeat with all other egg rolls.

6. Put rolls into air fryer, one batch at a time. Cook at the corresponding preset mode or Air Fry at 392°F (200°C) for 8 minutes.

7. Serve immediately.

Cheesy Beef Chuck Burgers

Prep time: 10 minutes | **Cook time**: 15 minutes | **Serves** 4

¾ pound (340 g) ground beef chuck

1 envelope onion soup mix

Kosher salt and freshly ground black pepper, to taste1 teaspoon paprika

4 slices Monterey Jack cheese4 ciabatta rolls

1. In a bowl, stir together the ground chuck, paprika, onion soup mix,

salt, and black pepper to combine well.

2. Take four equal portions of the mixture and mold each one into a

patty. Transfer to the air fryer and cook at the corresponding preset

mode or Air Fry at 385°F (196°C) for 10 minutes.

3. Put the slices of cheese on the top of the burgers.

4. Air fry for another minute before serving on ciabatta rolls.

Fast Chicken Fried Steak

Prep time: 15 minutes | **Cook time**: 10 minutes | **Serves** 4

½ cup flour

2 teaspoons salt, divided

Freshly ground black pepper, to taste

¼ teaspoon garlic powder

1 cup buttermilk

1 cup fine bread crumbs

4 (6-ounce / 170-g) tenderized top round steaks, ½-inch thick

Vegetable or canola oil

For the Gravy:

2 tablespoons butter or bacon drippings

¼ onion, minced

1 clove garlic, smashed

¼ teaspoon dried thyme

3 tablespoons flour

1 cup milk

Salt and freshly ground black pepper, to taste

Dashes of Worcestershire sauce

1. Set up a dredging station. Combine the flour, garlic powder, 1

teaspoon of salt, and black pepper in a shallow bowl. Pour the
buttermilk into a second shallow bowl. Finally, put the bread crumbs and 1 teaspoon of salt in a third shallow bowl.
2. Dip the tenderized steaks into the flour, then the buttermilk, and
then the bread crumb mixture, pressing the crumbs onto the steak.
Put them on a baking sheet and spray both sides generouslywith vegetable or canola oil.
3. Transfer the steaks to the air fryer basket, two at a time, and cook
at the corresponding preset mode or Air Fry at 400°F (204°C) for
10 minutes, flipping the steaks over halfway through the cookingtime. Hold the first batch of steaks warm in a 170°F (77°C) oven
while you air fry the second batch.
4. While the steaks are cooking, make the gravy. Melt the butter in a
small saucepan over medium heat on the stovetop. Add the onion,

garlic and thyme and cook for five minutes, until the onion is soft and just starting to brown. Stir in the flour and cook for another

five minutes, stirring regularly, until the mixture starts to brown.

Whisk in the milk and bring the mixture to a boil to thicken. Season to taste with salt, lots of freshly ground black pepper, and a

few dashes of Worcestershire sauce.

5. Pour the gravy over the chicken fried steaks and serve.

Crispy Pork Chop

Prep time: 10 minutes | **Cook time**: 20 minutes | **Serves** 4

1 tablespoon olive oil

¼ teaspoon ground black pepper

½ teaspoon salt

1 egg white

4 (4-ounce / 113-g) pork chops

¾ cup almond flour

2 sliced jalapeño peppers2

sliced scallions

2 tablespoons olive oil

¼ teaspoon ground white pepper

1 teaspoon sea salt

1. Coat the air fryer basket with olive oil.

2. Whisk egg white, salt, and black pepper together until foamy.

3. Cut pork chops into pieces, leaving just a bit on bones. Pat dry.

4. Add pieces of pork to egg white mixture, coating well. Letsit for

marinade 20 minutes.

5. Put marinated chops into a large bowl and add almond flour.

Dredge and shake off excess and place into air fryer.

6. Cook the chops at the corresponding preset mode or Air Fry at
360°F (182°C) for in the air fryer for 12 minutes.

7. Turn up the heat to 400°F (205°C) and air fry for another 6 minutes
until pork chops are nice and crisp.

8. Meanwhile, remove jalapeño seeds and chop up. Chop scallions
and mix with jalapeño pieces.

9. Heat a skillet with olive oil. Stir-fry the white pepper, salt, scallions, and jalapeños 60 seconds. Then add fried pork pieces to
skills and toss with scallion mixture. Stir-fry 1 to 2 minutes until
well coated and hot. 10. Serve immediately.

Casseroles, Frittatas, and Quiches

Sweet Peaches with Yogurt and Blueberries

Prep time: 10 minutes | **Cook time**: 7 to 11 minutes | **Serves** 6

3 peaches, peeled, halved, and pitted
2 tablespoons packed brown sugar
1 cup plain Greek yogurt
¼ teaspoon ground cinnamon
1 teaspoon pure vanilla extract
1 cup fresh blueberries

1. Arrange the peaches in the air fryer basket, cut-side up. Top with a generous sprinkle of brown sugar.
2. Cook at the corresponding preset mode or Air Fry at 380°F (193°C) for 7 to 11 minutes, or until the peaches are lightly browned and caramelized.
3. Meanwhile, whisk together the cinnamon, yogurt, and vanilla in a small bowl until smooth.
4. Remove the peaches from the basket to a plate. Serve topped with the yogurt mixture and fresh blueberries.

Honey Peaches and Apple Crumble

Prep time: 10 minutes | **Cook time**: 10 to 12 minutes | **Serves** 4

2 peaches, peeled, pitted, and chopped1

apple, peeled and chopped

2 tablespoons honey

½ cup quick-cooking oatmeal

⅓ cup whole-wheat pastry flour

2 tablespoons unsalted butter, at room temperature

3 tablespoons packed brown sugar

½ teaspoon ground cinnamon

1. Mix together the peaches, apple, and honey in a baking pan until
well incorporated.

2. In a bowl, combine the oatmeal, pastry flour, butter, brown sugar,
and cinnamon and stir to mix well. Spread this mixtureevenly over
the fruit.

3. Place the baking pan in the air fryer basket and cook at the

corresponding preset mode or Air Fry at 380°F (193°C) for 10 to
12 minutes, or until the fruit is bubbling around the edgesand the
topping is golden brown.
4. Remove from the basket and serve warm.

Golden Strawberry and Rhubarb Crisp

Prep time: 10 minutes | **Cook time**: 12 to 17 minutes | **Serves** 6

1½ cups sliced fresh strawberries

⅓ cup sugar

¾ cup sliced rhubarb

½ cup whole-wheat pastry flour

⅔ cup quick-cooking oatmeal

¼ cup packed brown sugar

½ teaspoon ground cinnamon

3 tablespoons unsalted butter, melted

1. Stir together the strawberries, sugar, and rhubarb in a baking pan.

2. Thoroughly combine the pastry flour, brown sugar, oatmeal, and
cinnamon in a medium bowl. Drizzle the melted butter over the flour mixture and stir until crumbly. Scatter the crumbly topping over the strawberry mixture.

3. Put the baking pan in the air fryer basket and cook at the

corresponding preset mode or Air Fry at 370°F (188°C) for 12 to
17 minutes, or until the fruit is bubbly and the topping is golden
brown.

4. Cool for 5 minutes and serve.

Fast Pumpkin Pudding with Vanilla Wafers

Prep time: 10 minutes | **Cook time**: 12 to 17 minutes | **Serves** 4

1 cup canned no-salt-added pumpkin purée (not pumpkin pie filling)

¼ cup packed brown sugar

3 tablespoons all-purpose flour

1 egg, whisked

2 tablespoons milk

1 tablespoon unsalted butter, melted1

teaspoon pure vanilla extract

4 low-fat vanilla wafers, crumbled

Nonstick cooking spray

1. Coat a baking pan with nonstick cooking spray. Set aside.

2. Mix the pumpkin purée, brown sugar, whisked egg, flour, melted

butter, milk, and vanilla in a medium bowl and whisk to combine.

Transfer the mixture to the baking pan.

3. Place the baking pan in the air fryer basket and cook at the corresponding preset mode or Air Fry at 350°F (177°C) for 12 to

17 minutes until set.

4. Remove the pudding from the basket to a wire rack to cool.

5. Divide the pudding into four bowls and serve with the vanilla

wafers sprinkled on top.

Cocoa Brownies

Prep time: 5 minutes | **Cook time**: 20 to 22 minutes | **Serves** 8

1 stick butter, melted

1 cup Swerve

2 eggs

1 cup coconut flour

½ cup unsweetened cocoa powder

2 tablespoons flaxseed meal

1 teaspoon baking powder

1 teaspoon vanilla essence

A pinch of salt

A pinch of ground cardamom

Cooking spray

1. Spray a baking pan with cooking spray.

2. Beat together the melted butter and Swerve in a large mixing dish
until fluffy. Whisk in the eggs.

3. Add the coconut flour, cocoa powder, baking powder, flaxseed
meal, vanilla essence, salt, and cardamom and stir with a spatula until well incorporated. Spread the mixture evenly into the

prepared baking pan.

4. Place the baking pan in the air fryer basket and cook at the corresponding preset mode or Air Fry at 350°F (177°C) for 20 to 22 minutes, or until a toothpick inserted in the center comes out clean.

5. Remove from the basket and place on a wire rack to cool completely. Cut into squares and serve immediately.

Easy White Chocolate Cookies

Prep time: 5 minutes | **Cook time**: 11 minutes | **Serves** 10

8 ounces (227 g) unsweetened white chocolate

2 eggs, well beaten

¾ cup butter, at room temperature

1⅔ cups almond flour

½ cup coconut flour

¾ cup granulated Swerve2

tablespoons coconut oil

⅓ teaspoon grated nutmeg

⅓ teaspoon ground allspice

⅓ teaspoon ground anise star

¼ teaspoon fine sea salt

1. Line the air fryer basket with parchment paper.

2. Combine all the ingredients in a mixing bowl and knead for about

3 to 4 minutes, or until a soft dough forms. Transfer to the refrigerator to chill for 20 minutes.

3. Make the cookies: Roll the dough into 1-inch balls and transfer to

parchment-lined basket, spacing 2 inches apart. Flatten eachwith the back of a spoon.

4. Cook at the corresponding preset mode or Air Fry at 350°F (177°C) for about 11 minutes until the cookies are golden and firm to the touch.

5. Transfer to a wire rack and let the cookies cool completely. Serve immediately.

Honey-Lemon Mixed Berry Crisp

Prep time: 10 minutes | **Cook time**: 11 to 16 minutes | **Serves** 4

½ cup fresh blueberries

½ cup chopped fresh strawberries

⅓ cup frozen raspberries, thawed

1 tablespoon honey

1 tablespoon freshly squeezed lemon juice

⅔ cup whole-wheat pastry flour

3 tablespoons packed brown sugar

2 tablespoons unsalted butter, melted

1. Place the strawberries, blueberries, and raspberries in a baking pan
and drizzle the honey and lemon juice over the top.

2. Combine the pastry flour and brown sugar in a small mixing bowl.

3. Add the butter and whisk until the mixture is crumbly. Scatter the
flour mixture on top of the fruit.

4. Put the baking pan in the air fryer basket and cook at the corresponding preset mode or Air Fry at 380°F (193°C) for 11 to 16

minutes, or until the fruit is bubbly and the topping is goldenbrown.

5. Remove from the basket and serve on a plate.

Golden Savory Blackberry Muffins

Prep time: 5 minutes | **Cook time**: 12 minutes | **Serves** 8

½ cup fresh blackberries

Dry Ingredients:

1½ cups almond flour

1 teaspoon baking powder

½ teaspoon baking soda

½ cup Swerve

¼ teaspoon kosher salt

Wet Ingredients:

2 eggs

¼ cup coconut oil, melted

½ cup milk

½ teaspoon vanilla paste

1. Line an 8-cup muffin tin with paper liners.

2. Thoroughly combine the almond flour, baking powder, baking soda, Swerve, and salt in a mixing bowl.

3. Whisk together the eggs, milk, coconut oil, and vanilla in a separate mixing bowl until smooth.

4. Add the wet mixture to the dry and fold in the blackberries. Stir with a spatula just until well incorporated.

5. Spoon the batter into the prepared muffin cups, filling each about
three-quarters full.

6. Cook at the corresponding preset mode or Air Fry at 350°F (177°C)
for 12 minutes, until the tops are golden and a toothpick inserted in
the middle comes out clean.

7. Allow the muffins to cool in the muffin tin for 10 minutes before
removing and serving

Mixed Berry Crumble

Prep time: 5 minutes | **Cook time**: 35 minutes | **Serves** 6

2 ounces (57 g) unsweetened mixed berries

½ cup granulated Swerve

2 tablespoons golden flaxseed meal1

teaspoon xanthan gum

½ teaspoon ground cinnamon

¼ teaspoon ground star anise

Topping:

½ stick butter, cut into small pieces1

cup powdered Swerve

⅔ cup almond flour

⅓ cup unsweetened coconut, finely shredded

½ teaspoon baking powder

Cooking spray

1. Coat 6 ramekins with cooking spray.

2. In a mixing dish, stir together the mixed berries, cinnamon,

granulated Swerve, xanthan gum, flaxseed meal, star anise. Divide

the berry mixture evenly among the prepared ramekins.

3. Combine the remaining ingredients in a separate mixing dish and
stir well. Scatter the topping over the berry mixture.
4. Working in batches, place the ramekins in the air fryer basket.
Cook at the corresponding preset mode or Air Fry at 330°F (166°C)
for 35 minutes until the topping is golden brown.
5. Serve warm.

Blackberry and Peach with Vanilla

Prep time: 10 minutes | **Cook time**: 20 minutes | **Serves** 4

Filling:

1 (6-ounce / 170-g) package blackberries

1½ cups chopped peaches, cut into ½-inch thick slices

2 teaspoons arrowroot or cornstarch

2 tablespoons coconut sugar

1 teaspoon lemon juice

Topping:

2 tablespoons sunflower oil

1 tablespoon maple syrup

1 teaspoon vanilla

3 tablespoons coconut sugar

½ cup rolled oats

⅓ cup whole-wheat pastry flour

1 teaspoon cinnamon

¼ teaspoon nutmeg

⅛ teaspoon sea salt

Make the Filling:

1. Combine the peaches, blackberries, arrowroot, coconut sugar, and

lemon juice in a baking pan.

2. Using a rubber spatula, stir until well incorporated. Set aside.

Make the Topping:

3. Combine the oil, maple syrup, and vanilla in a mixing bowl and stir

well. Whisk in the remaining ingredients. Spread this mixtureevenly over the filling.

4. Place the pan in the air fryer basket and cook at the correspondingpreset mode or Air Fry at 320°F (160°C) for 20 minutes, or until

the topping is crispy and golden brown. Serve warm

Breaded Bananas with Chocolate Sauce

Prep time: 10 minutes | **Cook time**: 10 minutes | **Serves** 6

¼ cup cornstarch

¼ cup plain bread crumbs

1 large egg, beaten

3 bananas, halved crosswise

Cooking spray

Chocolate sauce, for serving

1. Place the bread crumbs, cornstarch, and egg in three separate bowls.
2. Roll the bananas in the cornstarch, then in the beaten egg, and finally in the bread crumbs to coat well.
3. Spritz the air fryer basket with the cooking spray.
4. Arrange the banana halves in the basket and mist them with the cooking spray. Cook at the corresponding preset mode or Air Fry at 350°F (177°C) for 5 minutes. Flip the bananas and continue to air fry for another 2 minutes.

5. Remove the bananas from the basket to a serving plate. Serve with

the chocolate sauce drizzled over the top.

Chocolate Cinnamon S'mores

Prep time: 5 minutes | **Cook time**: 10 minutes | Makes 12 s'mores

12 whole cinnamon graham crackers, halved

2 (1.55-ounce / 44-g) chocolate bars, cut into 12 pieces12 marshmallows

1. Working in batches, arrange 6 graham cracker squares in the air fryer basket in a single layer.

2. Top each square with a piece of chocolate and bake for 2 minutes.

3. Remove the basket and place a marshmallow on each piece of melted chocolate. Cook at the corresponding preset mode or Air Fry at 350°F (177°C) for another 1 minute.

4. Remove from the basket to a serving plate. Repeat with the remaining 6 graham cracker squares, chocolate pieces, and marshmallows.

5. Serve topped with the remaining graham cracker squares

Simple Coconut Mixed Berry Crisp

Prep time: 5 minutes | **Cook time**: 20 minutes | **Serves** 6

1 tablespoon butter, melted

12 ounces (340 g) mixed berries

⅓ cup granulated Swerve

1 teaspoon pure vanilla extract

½ teaspoon ground cinnamon

¼ teaspoon ground cloves

¼ teaspoon grated nutmeg

½ cup coconut chips, for garnish

1. Coat a baking pan with melted butter.

2. Put the remaining ingredients except the coconut chips in the

prepared baking pan.

3. Cook at the corresponding preset mode or Air Fry at 330°F (166°C)

for 20 minutes.

4. Serve garnished with the coconut chips.

Fast Chocolate Peppermint Cheesecake

Prep time: 5 minutes | **Cook time**: 18 minutes | **Serves** 6

Crust:

½ cup butter, melted

½ cup coconut flour

2 tablespoons stevia

Cooking spray

Topping:

4 ounces (113 g) unsweetened baker's chocolate 1

cup mascarpone cheese, at room temperature 1

teaspoon vanilla extract

2 drops peppermint extract

1. Lightly coat a baking pan with cooking spray.

2. In a mixing bowl, whisk together the butter, flour, and stevia until

well combined. Transfer the mixture to the prepared bakingpan.

3. Place the baking pan in the air fryer and cook at the corresponding

preset mode or Air Fry at 350°F (177°C) for 18 minutes untila toothpick inserted in the center comes out clean.

4. Remove the crust from the air fryer to a wire rack to cool.

5. Once cooled completely, place it in the freezer for 20 minutes.

6. When ready, combine all the ingredients for the topping in a small

bowl and stir to incorporate.

7. Spread this topping over the crust and let it sit for another 15

minutes in the freezer.

8. Serve chilled.

Chocolate and Blueberry Cupcakes

Prep time: 5 minutes | **Cook time**: 15 minutes | **Serves** 6

¾ cup granulated erythritol

1¼ cups almond flour

1 teaspoon unsweetened baking powder3

teaspoons cocoa powder

½ teaspoon baking soda

½ teaspoon ground cinnamon

¼ teaspoon grated nutmeg

⅛ teaspoon salt

½ cup milk

1 stick butter, at room temperature

3 eggs, whisked

1 teaspoon pure rum extract

½ cup blueberries

Cooking spray

1. Spray a 6-cup muffin tin with cooking spray.

2. In a mixing bowl, combine the erythritol, cinnamon, nutmeg,
almond flour, cocoa powder, baking powder, baking soda, and salt
and stir until well blended.

3. In another mixing bowl, mix together the milk, butter, egg, and rum extract until thoroughly combined. Slowly and carefully pour this mixture into the bowl of dry mixture. Stir in the blueberries.

4. Spoon the batter into the greased muffin cups, filling each about three-quarters full.

5. Cook at the corresponding preset mode or Air Fry at 345°F (174°C) for 15 minutes, or until the center is springy and a toothpickinserted in the middle comes out clean.

6. Remove from the basket and place on a wire rack to cool. Serve immediately

VEGGIE

Fast Balsamic Brussels Sprouts

Prep time: 5 minutes | **Cook time**: 13 minutes | **Serves** 2

2 cups Brussels sprouts, halved

1 tablespoon olive oil

1 tablespoon balsamic vinegar1 tablespoon maple syrup

¼ teaspoon sea salt

1. Evenly coat the Brussels sprouts with the balsamic vinegar, maple syrup, olive oil, and salt.

2. Transfer to the air fryer basket and cook at the corresponding preset mode or Air Fry at 375°F (191°C) for 5 minutes. Give the basket a good shake, turn the heat to 400°F (204°C) and continue to cook for another 8 minutes.

3. Serve hot.

Ritzy Summer Rolls

Prep time: 15 minutes | **Cook time**: 15 minutes | **Serves** 4

1 cup shiitake mushroom, sliced thinly

1 celery stalk, chopped

1 medium carrot, shredded

½ teaspoon finely chopped ginger

1 teaspoon sugar

1 tablespoon soy sauce

1 teaspoon nutritional yeast

8 spring roll sheets

1 teaspoon corn starch

2 tablespoons water

1. In a bowl, combine the ginger, carrots, mushroom, soy sauce, celery, nutritional yeast, and sugar.
2. Mix the cornstarch and water to create an adhesive for the spring rolls.
3. Scoop a tablespoonful of the vegetable mixture into the middle of the spring roll sheets. Brush the edges of the sheets with the cornstarch adhesive and enclose around the filling to make spring

rolls.

4. Place the rolls inside the air fryer, and cook at the corresponding preset mode or Air Fry at 400°F (204°C) for 15 minutes or until crisp.

5. Serve hot.

Balsamic Rice and Eggplant Bowl

Prep time: 15 minutes | **Cook time**: 10 minutes | **Serves** 4

¼ cup sliced cucumber

1 teaspoon salt

1 tablespoon sugar

7 tablespoons Japanese rice vinegar3

medium eggplants, sliced

3 tablespoons sweet white miso paste1

tablespoon mirin rice wine

4 cups cooked sushi rice

4 spring onions

1 tablespoon toasted sesame seeds

1. Coat the cucumber slices with the rice wine vinegar, salt, and

sugar.

2. Put a dish on top of the bowl to weight it down completely.

3. In a bowl, mix the eggplants, miso paste, and mirin rice wine.

Allow to marinate for half an hour.

4. Put the eggplant slices in the air fryer and Cook at the corresponding preset mode or Air Fry at 400°F (204°C) for 10

minutes.

5. Fill the bottom of a serving bowl with rice and top with the

eggplants and pickled cucumbers.

6. Add the sesame seeds and spring onions for garnish. Serve immediately.

Veggies Pizza Squares

Prep time: 10 minutes | **Cook time**: 10 minutes | **Serves** 10

1 pizza dough, cut into squares

1 cup chopped oyster mushrooms

1 shallot, chopped

¼ red bell pepper, chopped

2 tablespoons parsley

Salt and ground black pepper, to taste

1. In a bowl, combine the oyster mushrooms, bell pepper, shallot, and

parsley. Sprinkle some salt and pepper as desired.

2. Spread this mixture on top of the pizza squares.

3. Cook at the corresponding preset mode or Air Fry at 400°F (204°C)

for 10 minutes.

4. Serve warm.

Cajun Sweet Potatoes with Tofu

Prep time: 15 minutes | **Cook time**: 35 minutes | **Serves** 8

8 sweet potatoes, scrubbed

2 tablespoons olive oil

1 large onion, chopped

2 green chilies, deseeded and chopped8 ounces (227 g) tofu, crumbled

2 tablespoons Cajun seasoning1 cup chopped tomatoes

1 can kidney beans, drained and rinsed

Salt and ground black pepper, to taste

1. With a knife, pierce the skin of the sweet potatoes and cook at the

corresponding preset mode or Air Fry at 400°F (204°C) for 30

minutes or until soft.

2. Remove from the air fryer, halve each potato, and set to one side.

3. Over a medium heat, fry the chilies and onions in the olive oil in a

skillet for 2 minutes until fragrant.

4. Add the tofu and Cajun seasoning and cook at the corresponding

preset mode or Air Fry at 400°F (204°C) for a further 3 minutes

before incorporating the kidney beans and tomatoes. Sprinkle some

salt and pepper as desire.

5. Top each sweet potato halve with a spoonful of the tofu mixture

and serve.

Cheesy Basmati Risotto

Prep time: 10 minutes | **Cook time**: 30 minutes | **Serves** 2

1 onion, diced

1 small carrot, diced

2 cups vegetable broth, boiling

½ cup grated Cheddar cheese

1 clove garlic, minced

¾ cup long-grain basmati rice

1 tablespoon olive oil

1 tablespoon unsalted butter

1. Grease a baking tin with oil and stir in the garlic, onion, carrot, and
butter.
2. Put the tin in the air fryer and cook at the corresponding preset
mode or Air Fry at 390°F (199°C) for 4 minutes.
3. Pour in the rice and cook at the corresponding preset mode or Air
Fry at 390°F (199°C) for a further 4 minutes, stirring three times
throughout the baking time.
4. Turn the temperature down to 320°F (160°C).

5. Add the vegetable broth and give the dish a gentle stir. Cook for 22

minutes, leaving the air fryer uncovered.

6. Pour in the cheese, stir once more and serve.

Classic Mediterranean Baked Eggs with Spinach

Prep time: 10 minutes | **Cook time**: 8 to 12 minutes | **Serves** 2

2 tablespoons olive oil

4 eggs, whisked

5 ounces (142 g) fresh spinach, chopped

1 medium-sized tomato, chopped

1 teaspoon fresh lemon juice

½ teaspoon ground black pepper

½ teaspoon coarse salt

½ cup roughly chopped fresh basil leaves, for garnish

1. Generously grease a baking pan with olive oil.
2. Stir together the remaining ingredients except the basil leaves in the greased baking pan until well incorporated.
3. Place the baking pan in the air fryer and cook at the corresponding preset mode or Air Fry at 280°F (137°C) for 8 to 12 minutes, or until the eggs are completely set and the vegetables are tender.
4. Serve garnished with the fresh basil leaves.